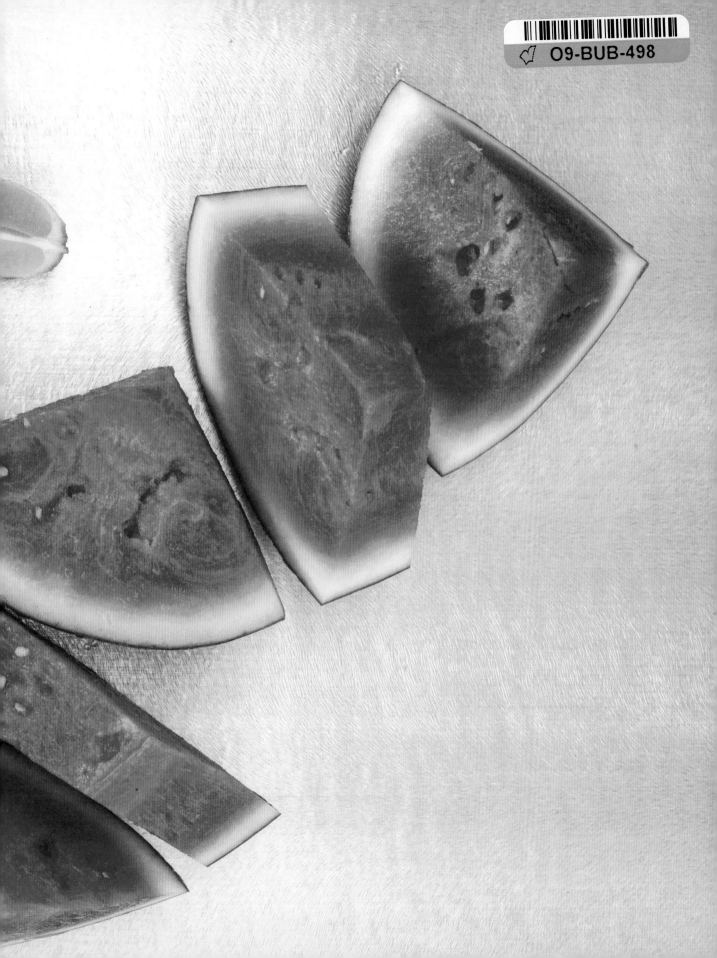

The Juice Bar

The Juice Bar

Sara Lewis

This edition published by Parragon Books Ltd in 2013 and
distributed by

Parragon Inc.
440 Park Avenue South, 13th Floor
New York, NY 10016
www.parragon.com/lovefood

LOVE FOOD is an imprint of Parragon Books Ltd

ISBN: 978-1-4723-2553-2

Printed in China

Created and produced by Pene Parker and Becca Spry
Author and food stylist: Sara Lewis
Photographer: Haraala Hamilton

Notes for the reader
This book uses standard kitchen measuring spoons and cups.
All spoon and cup measurements are level unless otherwise
indicated. Unless otherwise stated, milk is assumed to be whole,
eggs are large, individual vegetables are medium, and pepper
is freshly ground black pepper. The publisher recommends
consulting a physician or other healthcare professional before
embarking on major dietary changes. The publisher disclaims
any liability, loss, or risk that may be claimed or incurred
as a consequence—directly or indirectly—of the use and/or
application of any of the contents of this publication. While
the author has made every effort to ensure the information
contained in this book is accurate and up-to-date at the time
of publication, medical and pharmaceutical knowledge is
constantly changing. Pregnant and breastfeeding women are
advised to avoid eating peanuts and peanut products. People
with nut allergies should be aware that some of the prepared
ingredients used in the recipes in this book may contain nuts.
Always check the packaging before use.

The author would like to thank John Lewis for the loan
of the Vitamix liquidizer.

The juice bar

A juicer can help transform your health. With sugary cakes, high-salt and high-fat potato chips, and convenience meals within easy reach, along with the huge number of fast-food outlets, it is not surprising that levels of obesity, diabetes, heart disease, food allergies, digestive problems, asthma, and eczema are rising. Good health is priceless, so why do we fuel our bodies with such junk and wonder at the results? The secret of good health is to take small steps toward long-term healthy eating. Introducing a delicious juice or smoothie daily can help boost your energy, vitamin, and mineral levels and, in turn, improve the health of your skin, hair, eyes, and fingernails, as well as your mood and feeling of well-being.

Health benefits

Health professionals recommend that we eat five 2¾-ounce or more portions of fruit and vegetables per day (about one-third of our total daily food consumption). Yet the average consumption is nearer three portions, with only around 15 percent of people meeting the target. Studies show that people who eat plenty of fruit and vegetables have a lower risk of developing high blood pressure, heart disease, strokes, obesity, and some cancers.

It is estimated that diet will probably contribute to the development of approximately one-third of cancers. Eating more fruit and vegetables is the second most important cancer-prevention strategy after giving up smoking. Other health benefits include the delay in the onset of degenerative eye conditions, improved bone and digestive health, and reduced symptoms of asthma.

Juices are made using raw ingredients, so their nutritional content is high. Many vitamins and minerals are water-soluble, so they are lost when cooked in water, and a lot are destroyed by heat. When juiced, fruit and vegetables rehydrate the body and provide nutrients in a form that is easy to digest.

Fresh juices and smoothies energize you and can boost your sporting prowess. Smoothies, which are made in a blender with the whole, prepared fruit processed together, release energy into the body slowly, so they can help us to avoid the peaks and dips that may lead to mood swings.

Weight-loss program

Juices can play a key part in a weight-loss program. You can jump-start a diet by replacing two meals each day with a juice for just two days. After that time, only replace one meal each day with a juice. Alternatively, if you usually have a midmorning high-fat or high-sugar snack, or an evening glass of wine, simply choose a lower-calorie juice-based drink instead.

Juices for the family

We can all benefit from juice, from small kids bringing home colds and viruses, to youngsters battling hormones, exam stress, and acne, to stressed-out parents, to grandparents, to anyone recovering from illness. When giving juices to kids, if you don't let on what's in each drink, you'll be amazed at how many veggies you can sneak into them. Curly kale and broccoli are mild, especially when mixed with naturally sweet apple, pineapple, beet, or parsnip. The key is to get a good mixture of flavors. There are three main ways of making a juice: in an electric juicer, a blender, or by using a citrus press.

Electric juicers

Electric juicers have come a long way since the 1980s. You get what you pay for, so do your homework. If the price sounds too good to be true, then the machine may not have the muscle to do the job properly. Here are the things to consider when buying one.

What kind of juices do you want to make?
If you want to juice a mixture of fruit and vegetables, from root vegetables to green leafy vegetables, go for a mid-priced centrifugal juicer. These tall models look like a food processor and have a metal basket with teeth that spin around as you press foods through the chute. The juice is then collected in a pitcher, and the debris is collected in a pulp container.

If you want to juice your own wheatgrass and plenty of green leafy vegetables, then a masticating juicer is for you. These look a little like a grinding machine and work by crushing fruit and vegetables against a stainless-steel filter with a slowly rotating screw. They take longer to use, take time to clean, and the good ones tend to be expensive.

Blenders

Blenders vary greatly in motor power, speed settings, pitcher capacity, and price. Some of the more powerful models can crush ice, but not all, so check your manual before trying this. Their efficiency will greatly affect the texture of your juice, and because many kids and adults hate chunks, it might be worth upgrading to a better model if your machine lacks muscle.

For less powerful machines, chop fruit up small, especially pineapples and grapefruits, before blending. Put just a few pieces in the blender to begin with, then add the rest through the gap in the lid while the motor is running. Crush ice before adding, or stir cubes into a finished drink.

Smaller "personal" blenders with detachable drinking containers can be perfect for making a quick drink. Unscrew the blades and screw on the lid; you don't even need to decant the juice into a separate glass before drinking.

If using a blender, you will need to add liquid in the form of chilled water; rice, almond, or soy milk; yogurt; or juice. Food processors may be used in the same way, but they can have a bigger bowl, so are not always great for single servings.

How big is the chute? If you have a big chute, larger ingredients, such as apples, pears, and beets, can be added whole.

How many speeds are there? Two speeds are great: Choose low for fleshy fruit and vegetables, such as tomatoes, and high for hard fruit and vegetables, such as apples.

What about the pulp container? Choose one that is a good size, so that you don't have to empty it after you have made just one drink.

Is the machine easy to put together? If it's too difficult, you won't use it.

Can the machine go in the dishwasher? Okay, so the detachable parts of a juicer are bulky, and no one is suggesting that the motorized base should go in the dishwasher, but if you are rushing out to work in the morning and want to have a healthy juice, this could save you some vital minutes.

Handheld immersion blenders

These can be used for making blended juices. They are not suitable for blending hard ingredients, such as apples and root vegetables, but can work well if you press these ingredients through a juicer first and then blend the juice up with softer fruits, such as berries and grapes.

Citrus press

For the odd orange or lemon, a heavy glass, ceramic, or stainless-steel press or juicer with a ridged domed top will work fine. Choose one with a seed collector and moat or attached container to collect the juice. Dedicated cooks often like a small wooden reamer, but you will need a little bowl to catch the juice. Also available are chrome-plated free-standing extractors with a hinged arm that presses the fruit down onto the squeezer as the juice feeds into a cup below. A number of food processors come with a citrus juicer attachment, but if you plan to make more than one glass of juice at a time, consider buying a separate electric citrus juicer.

Extra accessories

Vegetable brush or new nail brush to scrub fruit and vegetables that don't need peeling.

Cutting board, good knife, and peeler.

Biodegradable food bags; add one to the pulp container when juicing.

Ice cube trays (unless you have a refrigerator that makes ice cubes and crushed ice). They are also great for freezing juice.

Choosing fruit & vegetables

As a rule of thumb, if the fruit or vegetables don't look good enough to eat, then they are not good enough to juice or blend. It can be tempting to use up that elderly banana or slightly battered pear in a juice, but resist the urge.

Glam up your glass

Citrus twists—cut a thin slice from an orange, lemon, or lime, then cut a slit into the center. Twist the slice and perch it on the glass.

Corkscrews—pare a long, thin strip of zest from an orange, lemon, or lime. Wrap it tightly around a toothpick, hold for a minute, then slide it off and drape the corkscrew over the glass.

Thin slices of zucchini or carrot can be pared from the length of the vegetable using a swivel-blade peeler. Insert a skewer in two places for a curved boat shape or roll it up tightly.

Foodie stirrers—try cinnamon sticks, halved lemongrass stems, or celery stalks.

Mini skewers—thread a few small pieces of fruit onto a toothpick, then rest it on the glass.

Salt or sugar kick—dip the top of the glass in lemon juice, then in salt or sugar.

How to use a juicer

Simply prepare fruit and vegetables and press them through the juicer. What could be easier? There's no need to add water, but you can if you want; it depends on the weather, how thirsty you are, and how strong the juice tastes.

Wheatgrass

Wheatgrass is difficult to juice unless you have a masticating juicer. It's potent, too, so don't try to drink too much in one go. If you juice it on its own, aim to serve just 3-tablespoon shots. Alternatively, stir 1 teaspoon of powdered wheatgrass into your juice; it may not contain quite as much nutrition, but it is easy to use.

Root vegetables

Sweet potatoes, beets, carrots, and parsnips just need a trim and a good scrub. There's no need to peel fresh ginger—just add it, skin and all. Depending on the width of your juicer chute, you may not even need to cut root vegetables into pieces.

Melons

Remove the skin from melons. There's no need to remove the seeds because the juicer can make superspeedy work of separating these.

Citrus fruit

Pare away the zest, leaving some of the pith on because it contains valuable nutrients. (You can leave some of the zest on lemons and limes for a tangy citrus hit if you prefer, but not on oranges or grapefruits.) If you want a thinner drink, squeeze the juice from the fruit and only add this.

Pineapples & kiwis

Remove the skin from pineapples, but there's no need to remove the eyes or core. You can leave the skin on kiwis, but the juice will not look as vibrant if you do.

Best for blending

The blender is best for softer fruit and vegetables. Avocados, tomatoes, bananas, soft juicy berries, and seedless grapes all work wonderfully and blend to a deliciously smooth drink in a blender. But you will need to add yogurt, or unsweetened soy, almond, or rice milk, or a splash of chilled water to help the blades spin around.

Prepare fruit and vegetables exactly as you would for a salad: Remove pits; peel off dark green, furry, or knobbly skins; and peel the zest from citrus fruit, but leave on some of the pith for extra fiber and a creamy texture. You don't need to skin tomatoes. Peel harder fruit, such as pineapples, and chop them into small pieces (there is no need to remove the core of a pineapple). Root vegetables, red cabbage, apples, and pears are too hard for blending, so must be fed through a juicer before being added to a blender and mixed with softer fruit and vegetables. Seeds and grains are best ground to a fine powder in a blender before you add them to a juice.

Softer vegetables & herbs

Soft vegetables, including bell peppers, broccoli florets, cabbage, celery, cucumber, kale, lettuce, tomatoes, and zucchini, and herbs should be added to the chute between solid vegetables or fruit where possible.

Papayas

Cut papayas in half and scoop out the seeds, then thinly cut the flesh away from the peel. They don't produce much juice.

Apples & pears

Wash apples and pears well, then juice them whole or cut them in half, if needed, to fit them into the juicer chute.

Mangoes

Cut a thick slice off the top and bottom of a mango to reveal the large, flat pit. Cut around this pit, pull away the flesh, and cut it from the skin. The fruit doesn't produce much juice, so mix it with melon, apple, or pineapple.

Jump-start

Muesli motivator

Refreshing and superzingy, this smoothie makes a delicious energy-packed breakfast. It will keep you feeling full until lunchtime, thanks to the natural fruit sugars and slow-release complex carbs from the grapefruit pith, rolled oats, and almonds.

Serves 1

* ¼ cup rolled oats
* ⅓ cup slivered almonds
* ½ ruby red grapefruit, zest and a little pith removed, seeded and coarsely chopped
* 1¼ cups raspberries
* 2 oranges, juice squeezed
* ½ cup chilled water

How to make it

Put the rolled oats and almonds in a blender and blend until finely ground. Add the grapefruit, raspberries, orange juice, and water, and blend until smooth. Pour into a glass and serve.

Nutty facts

Adding 1–2 tablespoons of almonds to a smoothie boosts its vitamin E, B vitamin, and protein levels, which is especially good news for vegetarians. Oats contain soluble fiber, and they and the grapefruit pith stimulate digestion and help remove cholesterol from the body.

Make it perfect!

Be sure to cut grapefruit up into small pieces before putting it in your blender so that you get a smooth juice.

Berry breakfast

This breakfast-in-a-glass is packed with sustaining nutrients to keep up your energy levels all morning.

Serves 1

* 1⅓ cups strawberries
* ¾ cup raspberries
* ½ cup unsweetened rice, almond, or soy milk
* ½ cup unsweetened muesli

To make this juice

Cut a strawberry in half and reserve one half. Remove the hulls from the remaining strawberries. Put the strawberries and raspberries in a blender and blend to a puree. Add the milk and muesli and blend until almost smooth. Pour into a glass, top with the reserved strawberry half, and serve.

Sensational strawberries

Strawberries have more vitamin C than any other red berries and so have great antiviral and antibacterial properties. They are rich in beta-carotene, which is converted by the body into vitamin A. Their natural fruit sugars also give the body an early morning energy boost. Strawberries contain lignin, which may help reduce blood cholesterol.

Say yes to soy!

Adding soy yogurt or soy milk to a juice is a great way to boost its protein levels. Many soy milks are fortified with vitamin D and calcium, which means they can also help strengthen bones and teeth. Choose soy yogurt or milk that is unsweetened. They are free of the milk sugar lactose, too.

Nutrient boosters

Fruit and vegetables are packed with nutrients —but add a few seeds, grains, or nuts to your juice or smoothie, and it will be an energy-lifting protein fix or vitamin and mineral power boost.

Nuts

Bursting with protein, just a tablespoon of nuts can give a boost to any fresh juice. Grind them in a blender, then add fruits and blend them, or store them in a jar in the refrigerator ready to stir into a juice. They are high in fat, which bumps up the calories, but they contain essential fatty acids, are rich in vitamin E, and include most of the B group of vitamins and a whole lot of minerals.

Wheat germ

Wheat germ is the small part inside a wheat grain, from which a plant grows. It should not be confused with wheat bran, which is the outer, fibrous part of the grain. It is packed with protein to aid muscle development, vitamin E to boost immunity and aid skin health, omega-3 fatty acids, zinc, magnesium, some of the B group of vitamins, and fiber. It is sold as flakes.

Oats

A great source of energy, oats' complex carbohydrates allow for them to be digested slowly and so help maintain sugar levels in the blood. Rich in soluble fiber, they help lower blood cholesterol levels, too. They are low in fat and a good source of protein. Grind in a blender, then blend with fruit and vegetables or stir into fresh juices. They contain avenin, a protein similar to gluten, which some gluten-intolerant people are also intolerant to.

Sesame, sunflower & pumpkin seeds

Each of these seeds contains protein, the B vitamins, vitamin E, and fiber. One tablespoon can contain as many as 100 calories, depending on which seed you choose, so they add an energy boost to drinks. They contain monounsaturated fats (good fats), too!

Ancient Aztecs believed that just 1 tablespoon of chia seeds could sustain a warrior for 24 hours.

Chia seeds

The new seeds on the block, chia deserve a special mention. Just 2 tablespoons can add valuable protein, fiber, and omega-3 and omega-6 fatty acids to a drink, not to mention calcium, iron, copper, and zinc. They're almost flavorless, so go unnoticed when ground and mixed into a juice. When combined with liquid, they form a gel, so help you feel full for longer.

Flaxseeds & hemp seeds

Sometimes called linseeds, golden or dark flaxseeds are rich in the B vitamins, magnesium, manganese, and omega-3 and omega-6 fatty acids. They are also high in fiber and phytochemicals, including antioxidants (although these are not found in the oil). Hemp seeds are the only seeds that contains all the essential amino acids, so they are a great source of protein.

Power-boosting beets

This robust, vibrant-color juice is packed with big flavors
and energy-boosting nutrients to get you going in the morning.

Serves 1

* 2 beets, halved
* 2 large carrots, halved
* 2 celery stalks, halved
* 2-inch piece of cucumber
* 2 red-skinned apples,
  such as Pippin, halved
* ¼ cup walnut pieces, finely ground
* small handful of ice (optional)

Mix it up

Cut two wafer-thin slices off one of the
beet halves and reserve. Feed the beet and
carrots, then the celery and cucumber, and
finally the apples through a juicer. Stir in the
walnuts. Fill a glass halfway with ice (if using),
then pour in the juice. Thread the beet slices
through a toothpick, lay it on top of the glass,
and serve immediately.

Sweet beet

Beet has one of the highest sugar
levels of any vegetable, with the
equivalent of 1 teaspoon of natural fruit
sugar in each 4-ounce portion of beets, so it
gives a great energy boost. It also contains
folates, vitamin C, and potassium, which
help to regulate blood pressure and
nerve function.

Beat the morning blues

Full of vitamin C-packed berries, this hearty juice is a truly supercharged breakfast immunity boost!

Serves 1

* 1 pear, halved
* 1 cup blueberries
* ½ cup soy yogurt
* ½ teaspoon agave syrup
* 2 teaspoons slivered almonds, toasted

Give it a whirl

Feed the pear through a juicer. Pour the juice into a blender, add the blueberries, and blend. Add the yogurt and agave syrup, and blend again until smooth. Pour into a glass, sprinkle with the almonds, and serve.

Agave syrup

The succulent agave plant, which is related to the yucca and lily, grows in the southern and western United States and in tropical South America. Agave syrup, extracted from agave plants, is sold in health food stores and is used as a sweetener. It is considered by many to be superior to sugar because, when compared to other sweeteners, it has a low-glycemic index, which means that it won't cause a sharp rise or fall in blood sugar when eaten.

Health notes

Our bodies need protein, which is found in almonds and soy yogurt, for the growth and repair of everything from muscles and bones to hair and fingernails. There's calcium and vitamin D in some fortified brands of soy yogurt, too. This breakfast-boosting drink also provides the minerals phosphorus, magnesium, and zinc, which are great for our bones and teeth.

Berry jump-start

This energizing, gorgeous-looking smoothie is a delicious and healthy way to jump-start your day.

Serves 1

* 1¼ cups blueberries
* 1 cup cranberries
* ⅔ cup plain yogurt
* 2 teaspoons honey
* ¼ cup chilled water

To make this smoothie

Put the blueberries and cranberries in a blender and blend until smooth. Add the yogurt, honey, and water, and blend again. Pour into a glass and serve.

Don't like honey & sugar? Try these ...

Honey supplies energy in the form of simple carbohydrates and is a mixture of fructose and glucose. The clearer the honey, the higher the fructose level. Sweet foods stimulate the brain to produce endorphins, the body's natural pain-killers. Agave syrup, brown rice syrup, and date syrup can all be used instead of honey. Agave syrup is naturally sweeter than honey. Brown rice syrup has a mild caramel flavor and is like maple syrup. Date syrup is a thick, concentrated puree of lightly cooked dates; you can make it by gently simmering dates with a little water, cinnamon, and vanilla, then pureeing and storing in the refrigerator.

Superfood: blueberries

Blueberries are packed with more antioxidants than many other fruit and vegetables. These antioxidants, called flavonoids, help to mop up damaging free radicals and to protect the body from premature aging, heart disease, cancer, and degenerative diseases. Forty blueberries (2¾ ounces) contain seven-and-a-half times more antioxidant activity than a small banana. They also contain vitamin C, which our body needs daily; natural fruit sugar for energy; and pectin, thought to help lower cholesterol and act as an anti-inflammatory.

Strawberry supercharge

The pomegranate is one of the oldest cultivated fruits and has been thought to symbolize health, fertility, and eternal life. This drink may not give you eternal life, but it will give you a supercharged vitamin boost to help you cope with the stresses of the day.

Serves 1

* 1½ cup hulled strawberries
* ½ large pomegranate, seeds only
* 2 crisp apples, such as Pippin, halved
* small handful of crushed ice (optional)

Give it a whirl

Feed the strawberries, pomegranate seeds, and apples through a juicer. Fill a glass halfway with crushed ice (if using), then pour in the juice and serve immediately.

Apples for concentration

After intense concentration at work or physical exercise, energy levels plummet. Apples provide natural sugars, which are absorbed more slowly than sugars found in manufactured glucose-rich energy drinks.

Green giant

Gently wake up with this beautiful, velvety-smooth, soothing juice. Think of it as a hug from the inside out! It looks and tastes good, and is packed with vitamins A, B, C, and E, plus the minerals iron and potassium.

Serves 1

* 1 apple, halved
* ½ cup green curly kale
* 2 kiwis, peeled
* 2 sprigs of fresh flat-leaf parsley
* ½ avocado, pitted and flesh scooped from the skin
* ¼ cup chilled water
* small handful of crushed ice (optional)

To make this juice

Feed the apple, then the kale and kiwis through a juicer. Pour the juice into a blender, add the parsley and avocado, and blend. Add the water and crushed ice, if using, and blend again, until smooth. Pour into a glass and serve immediately.

Green giant
page 29

Strawberry
supercharge
page 28

On your marks, get set, go!

Breakfast is arguably the most important meal of the day, and this shake includes a lot of vital nutrients. It's quick to make, tasty, and filling, but it won't leave you feeling heavy.

Serves 1

* 1½ tablespoons pumpkin seeds
* 2 tablespoons flaxseed
* 3 tablespoons slivered almonds
* 1 cup raspberries
* ¾ cup blueberries
* 1 cup vanilla soy yogurt
* ½ cup chilled water

Mix it up

Put the pumpkin seeds, flaxseed, and almonds in a blender, and blend until finely ground. Add the raspberries, blueberries, yogurt, and water, and blend until smooth. Pour into a glass and serve.

Quick banana boosters

Need to grab a quick breakfast? Then try these fab banana-base energy drinks. They're superquick, supersimple, and superhealthy!

1 Banana & blueberry

* 1 banana, peeled and coarsely chopped
* ¾ cup blueberries
* ½ cup unsweetened rice milk
* small handful of crushed ice

2 Banana & kiwi

* 1 banana, peeled and coarsely chopped
* 2 kiwis, peeled and coarsely chopped
* ½ cup unsweetened rice milk
* small handful of crushed ice

3 Banana & mango

* 1 banana, peeled and coarsely chopped
* ½ mango, pitted, peeled, and flesh coarsely chopped
* ½ cup unsweetened rice milk
* small handful of crushed ice

Serves 1

For each drink, put all the ingredients into a blender and blend until smooth. Pour into a glass and serve immediately.

Happiness is ... a banana!

Feeling a little down? Forget about chocolate, munch on a banana instead! It is the only fruit to contain the amino acid tryptophan plus vitamin B6, which together help the body produce serotonin (the natural chemical that helps to lift your mood). Naturally rich in fruit sugar and starch, bananas are great energy-boosting foods and have a high amount of potassium. They can help to regulate blood pressure, lower the risk of heart attacks and strokes, and reduce the risk of cancer.

Blackberry blaster

Banish those morning blues with this cinnamon-spiced, dairy-free juice. It's bursting with vitamins and minerals, and will keep you energized until lunchtime.

Serves 1

* 3 large red-skinned plums, halved and pitted
* ½ cup red curly kale
* 1 pear, halved
* ¾ cup blackberries
* 3 tablespoons wheat germ powder
* pinch of ground cinnamon (optional)
* small handful of crushed ice
* ¼–⅓ cup chilled water

Time to get started

Feed the plums, then the kale, and finally the pear through a juicer. Pour the juice into a blender. Add the blackberries (reserving one to decorate), wheat germ, cinnamon (if using), and crushed ice, and blend until smooth. Add the water to taste and blend again until smooth. Pour into a glass. Thread a blackberry through a toothpick, add it to the glass, and serve immediately.

Blackberries: nature's aspirin

Energy-boosting blackberries are a good source of vitamin C, folates, and fiber. More unusually, they also contain salicylates, a natural aspirin-like compound, so if you are allergic to aspirin, stay away from this fruit.

Vegetable belly treat

Wake up your body and stimulate your digestive system with this fresh-tasting orange-and-tomato drink. There is also a kick delivered by the chile, to shake up those taste buds!

Serves 1

* 3 oranges, zest and a little pith removed
* 1 carrot, halved
* 2 tomatoes, coarsely chopped
* ½ cup chilled water
* 1 small green chile, halved
* 2 celery stalks, thickly sliced
* 2 teaspoons hemp seed oil

Give it a whirl

Cut two oranges in half and feed them and the carrot through a juicer. Pour the juice into a blender. Coarsely chop and seed the remaining orange, then put it, the tomatoes, and water in the blender, and blend until smooth. Add the chile and celery, and blend again until blended. Pour into a glass, stir in the hemp seed oil, and serve.

Hurray for hemp seed oil

Hemp seed oil contains a good balance of both omega-3 and omega-6 fats. Health experts believe that it is the balance of these fats that is most important in maintaining health and protecting us from disease.

Carrot & ginger vitamin vitality

You don't need a partner for this kind of passion, just a couple of juicy passion fruit! Their delicately perfumed seeds add a touch of luxury to this otherwise simple juice. The fruits were originally called "grenadilla", but were renamed by Catholic missionaries, who thought their flowers looked like the crown of thorns that was placed on Christ's head.

Serves 1

* 3 large carrots, halved
* 2 passion fruits, seeds scooped out
* ½-inch piece of fresh ginger
* 2 crisp apples, halved
* 2 teaspoons wheat germ oil
* small handful of ice (optional)

How to make this juice

Feed the carrots, then the passion fruit seeds, then the ginger, and finally, the apples through a juicer. Stir in the oil. Fill a glass halfway with ice (if using), then pour in the juice and serve immediately.

Passion fruit power

The more wrinkled a passion fruit is, the sweeter the pulp will be. Each fruit contains up to 250 seeds packed into a juicy, aromatic sweet-sour yellow pulp that contains calcium, iron, and vitamins A and C.

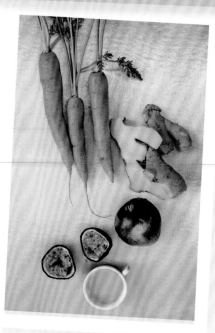

Peachy wake-up call

The sweet potato works wonderfully with the sweetness of the peach and fiery punch of the ginger, a fabulous way to shrug off early morning sluggishness!

Serves 1

* 1 sweet potato, cut into 4
* ½-inch piece of fresh ginger
* 3 carrots, halved
* 3 peaches, halved and pitted
* small handful of ice (optional)
* pinch of ground allspice, to serve (optional)

Mix it up

Feed the sweet potato and ginger, then the carrots, and finally, the peaches through a juicer. Fill a glass halfway with ice (if using), then pour in the juice. Sprinkle with the allspice (if using) and serve immediately.

Peachy
wake-up call
page 39

Carrot & ginger
vitamin vitality
page 38

Tropical sunrise & shine

Cheer up the dullest morning with this tropical fruit blend, and ramp up its nutrition with a sprinkling of chia seeds. If you're in a hurry, pack the juice into an insulated thermos, and enjoy it instead of a caffeine-loaded tea or coffee when you get to work.

Serves 1

* 3 tablespoons goji berries
* 1 tablespoon chia seeds
* ½ papaya, peeled, seeded, and coarsely chopped
* ¼ pineapple, peeled and coarsely chopped
* ½ lime, zest and a little pith removed, seeded and coarsely chopped
* 1 cup chilled water
* small handful of crushed ice (optional)

Bring me sunshine!

Put the goji berries and chia seeds in a blender, and blend until finely ground. Add the papaya, pineapple, lime, and water, and blend until smooth. Add the crushed ice (if using) and blend again, until blended. Pour into a glass and serve immediately.

Mango magic start-up

This beautiful smoothie is packed with powerful heart-protective and cancer-fighting antioxidants, plus vitamins B and C. Mangoes, oranges, and pomegranate seeds are all good sources of potassium, which helps to regulate blood pressure.

Serves 1

* ½ pomegranate, seeds only
* 1 mango, pitted, peeled, and coarsely chopped
* 1 orange, zest and a little pith removed, seeded and coarsely chopped

Go, man, go!

Reserve 1 tablespoon of the pomegranate seeds. Put the rest in a blender, and blend until combined, then pour into a glass. Put the mango and orange in the blender and blend until smooth. Pour onto the pomegranate juice, sprinkle with the reserved pomegranate seeds, and serve.

The power of pomegranate

It only takes a few minutes to pop the pomegranate seeds from the fruit, but they are nutrient-dense and contain high levels of flavonoids and polyphenols, potent antioxidants thought to help protect against heart disease and cancer. It's claimed that a glass of pomegranate juice contains more antioxidants than red wine, green tea, blueberries, and cranberries.

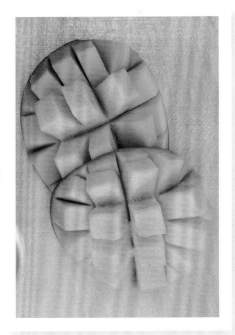

Red rouser

Get the day off to a fabulously fruity start with this irresistibly zingy and pretty juice!

Serves 1

* 1 apple, halved
* 2⅓ cups pitted cherries
* ⅔ cup red grapes
* ½ lime, zest and a little pith removed
* 2 tablespoons soy yogurt

Juice it up

Feed the apple, then the cherries, grapes, and lime through a juicer. Whisk in the yogurt. Pour into a glass and serve.

Gadget tip!

A cherry pitter is small and easy to store — and it makes taking the pits out of the fruit child's play!

Rehydrate

Go, children, go!

Start giving your children the healthy-eating message when they are young with these smoothies. The oranges are squeezed to make the smoothies extra smooth!

1

Strawberry & banana

* 1 cup strawberries, hulled
* 1 banana, peeled and coarsely chopped
* ½ orange, juice squeezed
* small handful of crushed ice
* chilled water, to taste

Serves 1

For each drink, put all the fruit and juice in a blender, and blend until smooth. Add the crushed ice and blend again. Pour into a glass, fill up with water to taste, and serve immediately.

Children's nutrition

Children need nutrient-dense foods to maintain energy levels and good fats from dairy foods for fat-soluble vitamins that are vital for growing bones and teeth. They need fiber, too, but not too much of it, or those tiny stomachs will fill up before enough protein, vitamins, and minerals have been consumed.

2

Avocado & grape

* ½ avocado, pitted and flesh scooped from the skin
* ¾ cup green seedless grapes
* ½ orange, juice squeezed
* small handful of crushed ice
* chilled water, to taste

Choosing a blender

Most kids hate chunks or pulp, so buy the best blender you can afford. Budget ones don't always make smooth drinks!

Juice benefits

Fruit and vegetable juices are great ways to sneak a lot of nutrients into your child's diet without him or her noticing. Serve with a sandwich for a healthy lunch.

3

Carrot & papaya

* ½ papaya, peeled, seeded, and coarsely chopped
* ½ orange, juice squeezed
* 2 carrots, halved and fed through a juicer
* small handful of crushed ice
* chilled water, to taste

Tantalizing tomato refresher

The success of this refreshing juice depends on the quality of the tomatoes; homegrown and freshly picked ones are perfect, but otherwise look for good, larger tomatoes with a deep color and sold on the vine for the best flavor.

Serves 1

* 2 carrots, halved
* 1 celery stalk, halved
* 1-inch slice of broccoli stem
* small handful of fresh basil leaves
* 4 tomatoes
* small handful of ice (optional)

Juice it up

Feed the carrots, then the celery, broccoli, and most of the basil, and finally, the tomatoes through a juicer. Fill a glass halfway with ice (if using), then pour in the juice. Garnish with the remaining basil and serve immediately.

How to juice herbs

To get the most juice from herbs, sandwich them between firmer fruit or vegetables, so that their weight helps to press down on the leaves as they go through the juicer chute.

Kiwi quencher

What a combo: cool, jewel-like kiwi fruits blended with naturally juicy green grapes and thirst-quenching lettuce.

Serves 1

* ½ romaine lettuce
* 4 kiwis, peeled
* ¾ cup green seedless grapes
* 1 large pear, halved
* small handful of ice, to serve (optional)

To make this juice

Peel off a lettuce leaf and reserve. Feed the kiwis and grapes, then the lettuce and pear through a juicer. Fill a glass halfway with ice (if using), then pour in the juice. Decorate with the reserved lettuce leaf and serve immediately.

Superfood: kiwis

A single kiwi contains more immune-boosting vitamin C than the recommended daily allowance and as much potassium as a small banana, helping to maintain fluid and electrolyte balance. They are rich in magnesium, which improves nerve and muscle function while boosting your energy levels, and zinc for healthy hair, skin, teeth, and nails. There's lutein, too, an antioxidant that seems to protect against macular degeneration (one of the leading causes of impaired vision in people over 50 years old).

Ruby fruit reviver

There's nothing more refreshing than a locally grown strawberry in the summer, but this smoothie can be enjoyed at any time of year— just shop carefully for the imported strawberries that really smell and taste as they should: Biggest doesn't necessarily mean best!

Serves 1

* 1 ruby red grapefruit, zest and a little pith removed, seeded, and coarsely chopped
* ¼ cucumber, coarsely chopped
* 1 cup hulled strawberries
* small handful of crushed ice (optional)

Great ruby grapefruits

Ruby grapefruits contain lycopene, an antioxidant thought to help protect the body against some cancers and lower the risk of heart disease. They're sweeter than white-flesh varieties and packed with vitamin C. In this drink, the strawberries also contain antioxidants and vitamin C, plus ellagic acid (which may help protect against collagen destruction and the inflammatory response after sun damage that can cause wrinkles).

Time for a revival

Put the grapefruit and cucumber in a blender, and blend until smooth. Add the strawberries and crushed ice (if using) and blend until blended. Pour into a glass and serve immediately.

Raspberry & watermelon crush

As the name suggests, watermelon is packed full of water, so what better way to rehydrate your body than with this delicately flavored smoothie blended with the natural sweetness of raspberries and a hint of lime?

Serves 1

* ¼ small watermelon, peeled, coarsely chopped, and most of the black seeds removed
* ½ lime, zest and most of the pith removed, seeded, and coarsely chopped
* 1 cup raspberries
* small handful of crushed ice (optional)

To make this smoothie

Put the watermelon and lime in a blender, and blend until smooth. Add the raspberries and crushed ice, if using, and blend again. Pour into a glass and serve immediately.

Minted melon drink

Quench your thirst with the lightest of fruit drinks. Forget sugar-loaded commercial drinks; this simple homemade one has just four ingredients plus ice and is additive-free.

Serves 1

* ½ honeydew melon, thickly sliced and peel removed
* 5 sprigs of fresh mint
* ½ lime, zest and a little pith removed
* 1-inch slice of broccoli stem
* small handful of crushed ice (optional)

Time to get started

Feed the melon and mint, then the lime and broccoli through a juicer. Fill a glass halfway with crushed ice (if using), then pour in the juice and serve immediately.

Give broccoli a chance

Broccoli is packed with beneficial phytochemicals, including indoles (nitrogen compounds that may help to prevent carcinogens from damaging DNA and so help to protect against cancer). It also contains vitamin C, beta-carotene, folate, iron, and potassium. The stem has just as many nutrients as the florets, yet it is often trashed.

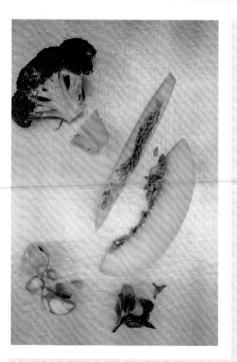

Cherry aid

Fresh cherries taste of pure summer. If you're short of time, use pitted frozen ones, but thaw them in the microwave or let them stand in the kitchen for half an hour before using, so that you can get the maximum juice out of them.

Serves 1

* 2 pears, halved
* 1 tablespoon chia seeds
* 1¼ cup pitted cherries
* ½ cup chilled water
* small handful of crushed ice (optional)

Mix it up

Feed the pears through a juicer. Put the chia seeds in a blender, and blend until finely ground. Add the pear juice, cherries, water, and crushed ice (if using), and blend until smooth. Pour into a glass and serve immediately.

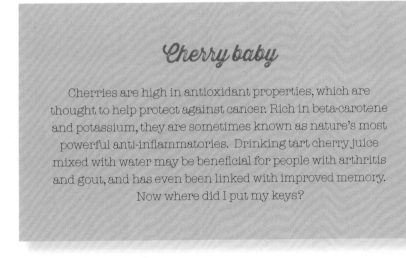

Cherry baby

Cherries are high in antioxidant properties, which are thought to help protect against cancer. Rich in beta-carotene and potassium, they are sometimes known as nature's most powerful anti-inflammatories. Drinking tart cherry juice mixed with water may be beneficial for people with arthritis and gout, and has even been linked with improved memory. Now where did I put my keys?

Minted melon drink

page 60

Summer corn quencher

Corn makes a delicious, creamy, smooth drink. Mix with juicy yellow bell pepper, naturally sweet apple, and a hint of cilantro, and you have a summer cocktail that will soothe the most parched of throats.

Serves 1

* 1 ear of corn, shucked
* 4 sprigs of fresh cilantro
* 1 yellow bell pepper, halved
* 1 apple, halved
* small handful of ice (optional)

Juice it up

Cut the kernels from the ear of corn, then feed them through a juicer. Feed the cilantro, then the bell pepper, and finally the apple through the juicer. Fill a glass halfway with ice (if using), then pour in the juice and serve.

Cherry aid

page 61

Dark beet thirst-quencher

Cool down on a hot day with this beautiful-looking thirst-quencher. The natural sweetness of the beet will make it surprisingly tempting for children as well as adults.

Serves 1

* 1 orange, seeded and zest and a little pith removed
* 2 cooked beets
* 3 tablespoons plain yogurt
* ⅓ cup chilled water
* small handful of ice (optional)

Give it a whirl

Remove a segment from the orange, cut it in half, and reserve, then coarsely chop the rest. Put the beets and orange in a blender, and blend until smooth. Add the yogurt and water, and blend again. Pour into a glass. Thread the orange pieces through a toothpick, lay it on top of the glass, and serve, with ice, if using.

Stay hydrated

Water makes up about 70 percent of our muscles and 75 percent of our brains. In everyday breathing, we lose about 2 cups of water, so it is important to keep the body hydrated all year round instead of just when the weather is hot. When we exercise, we lose more water through sweat. Caffeinated drinks, such as tea and coffee, and alcohol, all contain substances that cause dehydration.

Cool as a cucumber

This is like a cooling summer salad in a glass: light and fresh, with a gentle pepperiness from the arugula, a dash of mouth-freshening garden mint, and a hint of appley sweetness.

Serves 1

* ½ cucumber, halved
* ⅔ cup arugula
* 3 sprigs of fresh mint
* 1 zucchini
* 1 celery stalk, halved
* 1 apple, halved
* small handful of crushed ice (optional)

Go cucumber crazy!

Feed the cucumber, then the arugula and mint, and finally the zucchini, celery, and apple through a juicer. Fill a glass halfway with crushed ice (if using), then pour in the juice and serve immediately.

Water & your bowels

You need water not only to keep your body hydrated, but also to keep the bowels moving. The longer food waste stays in the colon, the more dehydrated and compacted it becomes and the more difficult it is to move. Aim to drink at least 7 cups of water each day; fresh juices will count, but don't overdo them, or you will have the opposite problem instead of constipation.

Celery choice

Not a fan of celery? Omit it and add a little more cucumber instead. If you do add it, remember that you can juice the leaves.

Fennel & tomato refresher

Aromatic fennel, fresh celery, and tomatoes, a zingy citrus hit and subtly sweet apple—this refreshing drink is great served any time of day or as a light lunch.

Serves 1

* 1 fennel bulb, halved
* 1 apple, halved
* 2 oranges, seeded and zest and a little pith removed, halved
* 2 celery stalks, halved
* 4 tomatoes
* small handful of crushed ice (optional)

On your marks, get set, go!

Feed the fennel and apple, then the oranges and celery, and finally, the tomatoes through a juicer. Fill a glass halfway with crushed ice (if using), then pour in the juice and serve immediately.

Cool as a
cucumber

page 66

Fennel
& tomato
refresher

page 67

Peach perfect rehydrator

Think of peach Melba blended into a foaming fruity drink; perfect on a balmy summer's afternoon. Why not pack this smoothie into an insulated thermos and enjoy it as part of a family picnic or quick lunch for one on a park bench?

Serves 1

* 3 tablespoons goji berries
* 2 peaches, halved, pitted, and coarsely chopped
* 1¼ cups raspberries
* 1 cup chilled water
* small handful of crushed ice

For a peach of a drink ...

Put the goji berries in a blender and blend until finely ground. Add all the remaining ingredients and blend until smooth. Pour into a glass and serve immediately.

Green steam

Because melon contains such a high proportion of water, it is great for rehydrating you. Honeydew melon has a light, delicate perfume and flavor. A ripe honeydew should have a bright, lemon-color skin, feel firm, but yield slightly when pressed, and have no soft spots. Galia and cantaloupe melons would also work well in this drink.

Serves 1

* 1⅓ cups sugar snap peas
* 2-inch piece of cucumber, plus a cucumber stick to garnish
* 2 kiwis, peeled
* ¼ honeydew melon, thickly sliced and peel removed
* 1 teaspoon spirulina powder (optional)
* 1 cup chilled water
* small handful of ice (optional)

Give it a whirl

Feed the sugar snap peas, cucumber, and kiwis, then the melon through a juicer. Stir in the spirulina powder (if using) and water. Fill a glass halfway with ice (if using), then pour in the juice and serve immediately with the cucumber stick as a stirrer.

New to spirulina?

Add spirulina as a protein-booster, and watch how it dramatically changes color from a fine white powder to a cartoon-style dark green. Made from a cultivated algae, it contains chlorophyll, vitamin E, the B group of vitamins, linolenic acid, calcium, iron, protein, and zinc. Look for it in packs in health food stores. (Also see page 122.)

Green
& pleasant juice
Spirulina makes this pea-green
juice turn extremely dark green.

Melon, pear & ginger spritzer

A refreshingly healthy version of ginger ale, with no chemicals and no added sugars, just 100 percent natural ingredients.

Serves 1

* ½ honeydew melon, thickly sliced and peel removed
* ½-inch piece of fresh ginger
* 1 pear, halved
* small handful of ice (optional)
* ½ cup sparkling mineral water, chilled

Time for a spritz

Feed the melon, then the ginger, and finally, the pear through a juicer. Fill a glass halfway with ice (if using), then pour in the juice. Add the sparkling mineral water and serve.

Berry booster

Think of this smoothie as the ultimate beauty treatment: It will rehydrate your skin and plump up and reduce those wrinkles, and the vitamin C-loaded berries will help clear up any acne and blemishes.

Serves 1

* 1 cup strawberries
* ¾ cup raspberries
* ⅔ cup blackberries
* ¾ cup chilled water
* small handful of ice (optional)

Berry bonus

We all know that summer berries contain vitamin C, but did you know that raspberries contain manganese, which assists with the metabolism of carbohydrates, proteins, and cholesterol and helps to keep our bones healthy? Berries are also great for keeping your digestive tract in good health; their tiny fibrous seeds help keep our food moving through the body and prevent constipation.

Now for the blender ...

Cut a strawberry in half and reserve one half along with a raspberry and a blackberry. Remove the hulls from the remaining strawberries. Put the strawberries, raspberries, blackberries, and water in a blender, and blend until smooth. Fill a glass halfway with ice (if using), then pour in the juice. Thread the fruit onto a wooden skewer to make a stirrer, then serve with the juice.

Fab frozen berries!
Keep a supply of berries in the freezer. Let them defrost slightly or partly thaw in the microwave before blending them into a juice.

Lychee & pineapple pep-up

Create a drink with a taste of Southeast Asia, using fragrant lemongrass and lychees blended with pineapple and melon.

Serves 1

* 1½ lemongrass stalks
* ¼ cup boiling water
* 6 lychees, peeled and pitted
* ½ small pineapple, peeled and cut into thick slices
* ¼ honeydew melon, thickly sliced and peel removed
* small handful of ice (optional)

To make this juice

Cut the whole lemongrass stalk in half lengthwise, then crosswise. Bruise it with a rolling pin to release its flavor, then put it in a shallow bowl and add the boiling water. Cover it and let it go cold, then drain and reserve the soaking water. Feed the softened lemongrass, lychees, and pineapple, then the melon through a juicer. Mix in the reserved soaking water. Fill a glass halfway with ice (if using), then pour in the juice and serve immediately with the remaining half lemongrass stalk as a stirrer.

Stay hydrated for sports

It's especially important to keep fluid levels up pre- and post-sports. Drinking a healthy juice before any physical activity may keep your heart rate and body temperature lower.

Citrus refresher

Not for the fainthearted, this fresh, zingy smoothie will certainly wake you up if you're having a midmorning slump.

Serves 1

* 1 pink grapefruit, zest and a little pith removed, seeded, and coarsely chopped
* 1 orange, zest and a little pith removed, seeded, and coarsely chopped
* ½ lemon, zest and pith removed, seeded, and coarsely chopped
* ½ lime, zest and pith removed, seeded, and coarsely chopped, plus 1 slice to decorate

Blend it up

Put all the ingredients in a blender and blend until smooth. Pour into a glass, decorate with the slice of lime, and serve.

Cut down on caffeine

Most of us drink far too much caffeine-loaded tea and coffee. Instead of quenching your thirst, it can lead to dehydration and reduce your stimulus to drink. In fact, caffeine drinks shouldn't even be counted as part of your daily fluid intake requirement. Once you start choosing homemade, superhealthy, rehydrating juices, you will see a difference. They not only boost fluid levels, but also supercharge the body's nutrient levels in one easy-to-digest hit.

Energy

Energy-boosting facts

If you need a quick energy boost, make your juice rich in naturally sweet fruit, such as apples, oranges, and berries. For a sustained boost, choose fruit and vegetables with less sugar and more starch, such as beets, bananas, and avocados, plus ground grains and seeds.

Types of carbohydrates

Carbohydrates supply energy to the body. The digestive system converts them into glucose (blood sugar), and this is then carried in the blood and used for energy. Carbohydrates can be broken down into three groups: sugar, starch, and fiber.

Sugar

Try to focus your sugar consumption on natural sugars found in fruit and vegetables instead of refined sugars found in cookies, cakes, pastries, jellies, preserves, soft drinks, candies, and many other prepared foods.

Starch

Good sources of starch include bananas, parsnips, sweet potatoes, carrots, beets, corn, and whole-grain cereals. Refined starches (the baddies) are found in cookies, pastries, cakes, sugary breakfast cereals, white bread, pasta, and rice, among other foods.

Fiber

Fiber is found in fruit and vegetables, cereals (especially whole-grain ones), dried beans, nuts, and seeds.

Sugar overload

The pancreas secretes insulin, and this controls your body's uptake of glucose (blood sugar). If your diet is too high in sugar, you can upset the delicate balance of your blood-sugar level, causing fluctuations in energy and mood that can make you feel tired and irritable. The excess sugar is then stored in the liver as glycogen and as fat around the body.

Juices after exercise

If we have too little energy, we may tire quickly, lose concentration, and have delayed recovery. Therefore, after exercise, it is important to boost our energy levels, and a freshly made juice is a good way to do this. The most effective refueling occurs within 30 minutes of exercise.

What is an isotonic drink?

An isotonic drink is a sports drink used to replace fluids and electrolytes and has a similar concentration to the body's own fluids. Generally made up of glucose and water, isotonic drinks contain added vitamins and salts to compensate for those lost during sweating. Typically, they contain between four and eight percent carbohydrates to improve stamina. They are usually commercially made, but they can be homemade with an equal mix of fresh fruit or vegetable juice and water, and a pinch of salt.

Hypertonic drinks contain between 10 and 15 percent carbohydrates and rarely contain electrolytes. The higher the level of carbohydrates in a drink, the greater the energy boost and the slower the stomach will empty, reducing urine output and encouraging fluid retention. They should be consumed only during and after endurance events, such as a marathon run, but make sure you follow up with water to rehydrate later. Choose fruit smoothies or drinks made with whole fruits or vegetables, such as bananas, avocados, or beets, and soy yogurt or milk.

Hypotonic drinks are intended to quickly replace water lost during sweating. They do not generally contain carbohydrates, but they do contain sodium and potassium, which tend to be lost when we sweat.

Water to aid concentration

Ever sat at your desk and struggled to concentrate? Then it might not just be an energy boost you need. Water and natural fruit juices are also essential. Your brain is made up of 75 percent water, so keeping hydrated is vital. When you are dehydrated, your concentration can decrease by 13 percent and your short-term memory by seven percent, so keep your fluid levels up—especially when studying for an exam. We also need water to help maintain normal blood pressure and body temperature. It is important to drink plenty of fluids, even when you don't feel thirsty, especially in hot weather or after exercise. Aim for a mixture of fresh juices or water instead of caffeine-loaded tea or coffee, which can dehydrate, or sugary commercial drinks.

Blueberry blast

The blueberry is a superhero in the food world. When mixed with pear, plain yogurt, and thirst-quenching chilled water, as in this drink, it will get you through the most hectic of schedules. You can use two apples instead of the water if you prefer; just juice them with the pear.

Serves 1

* 1 pear, halved
* ¾ cup blueberries
* ¾ cup plain yogurt
* 3 tablespoons wheat germ
* ¾ cup chilled water
* small handful of crushed ice (optional)

How to make it

Feed the pear through a juicer. Pour the juice into a blender, add the blueberries, yogurt, wheat germ, and water, and blend. Add the crushed ice (if using) and blend again, until smooth. Pour into a glass and serve immediately.

Blueberries: good mood food

The antioxidant power of blueberries has been shown to help stabilize brain function and protect the neural tissue from oxidative stress—which may improve memory and learning and reduce the symptoms of depression.

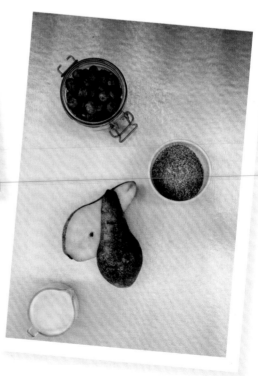

Keep it for later ...
If you don't drink this all at once, the wheat germ tends to swell, so you might need to add an extra splash of water when you finish it later.

Single-shot sports boosters

Have one of these potent juices just before you start strenuous exercise for a vitamin and mineral boost to energize muscles and aid performance. Transport them to the gym in a well-sealed insulated thermos.

Serves 1

Beet booster
* 2 beets, halved
* ¼ cup chilled water (optional)

Kiwi booster
* 2 kiwis

Blueberry booster
* 1 cup blueberries
* ¼ cup chilled water

To make these juices

* For the Beet booster, feed the beets through a juicer. Pour into a glass, add the water (if using), and serve.

* For the Kiwi booster, feed the kiwis through a juicer. Pour into a glass and serve.

* For the Blueberry booster, put the blueberries and water in a blender, then blend until smooth. Pour into a glass and serve.

Water versus juices

When you exercise, you lose many of the minerals in your body through sweat. Water alone will rehydrate you, but so can juices. Homemade fruit and vegetable juices also boost your energy, increase your vitamin and mineral intake, and help you rehydrate more quickly, speeding up recovery time. But best of all is to drink a mixture of the two in a homemade isotonic sports drink.

Raspberry rejuvenator

Raspberries and bananas give the body a slowly released energy boost to reenergize you in a sustained way.

Serves 1

* ¼ cup goji berries
* 1 small banana, peeled and coarsely chopped
* 1 cup raspberries
* 2 oranges, juice squeezed
* small handful of crushed ice (optional)
* chilled water, to taste

Blend it up

Put the goji berries in a blender and blend until finely ground. Add the banana, raspberries, and orange juice, and blend again. Add the crushed ice (if using) and blend again, until smooth. Add water to taste, pour into a glass, and serve immediately.

Balancing your carbs & protein

For sportsmen and sportswomen, it's particularly important to get the right mixture of protein and carbohydrates. Too few carbs and your low energy levels will make it difficult for you to train and perform at your best, and your body will use any protein in your food and drink for energy instead of for building muscles.

Juicing oranges

Oranges vary greatly in the amount of juice that they produce. If they are kept at room temperature, they will be easier to squeeze. Adjust this juice with water as needed.

Pink energy

Freshly blended, exotically fragrant papaya, as well as strawberries and lime, make this a zingy drink. The addition of soy milk makes it easy to digest and boosts energy.

Serves 1

* ½ papaya, peeled, seeded, and coarsely chopped
* 1 cup hulled strawberries
* 1 banana, peeled and coarsely chopped
* ½ lime, juice squeezed
* 1 cup unsweetened rice, almond, or soy milk
* small handful of crushed ice (optional)

On your marks, get set, go!

Put the papaya, strawberries, and banana in a blender and blend. Add the lime juice and milk, and blend again. Add the crushed ice (if using) and blend again, until smooth. Pour into a glass and serve.

Papaya for pain relief

Papaya contains the enzyme papain, which is similar to pepsin (produced by the digestive system to break down proteins). It also exhibits pain-relieving properties, so helps to soothe your stomach, and inflammation and muscle pain after exercise. Half a medium fruit will provide an adult's daily allowance of vitamin C and contains beta-carotene and small amounts of calcium and iron.

Turbo express

This smoothie includes everything you need to revitalize your body after a strenuous workout: rehydrating melon, energy-boosting banana, vitamin C-packed grapes, and iron-rich watercress—you're set!

Serves 1

* ¼ honeydew melon, seeded, peeled, and coarsely chopped
* 1 banana, peeled and coarsely chopped
* 1 kiwi, peeled and coarsely chopped
* ¾ cup green seedless grapes
* small handful of watercress (optional)
* ½ cup unsweetened rice, almond, or soy milk
* small handful of crushed ice (optional)

Now blend your smoothie!

Put the melon, banana, kiwi, grapes, and watercress (if using) in a blender and blend. Add the milk and crushed ice (if using) and blend again, until smooth. Pour into a glass and serve.

Wow, watercress!

Watercress is packed with antioxidants, minerals, and vitamins C and K. It's also rich in chlorophyll, which assists with oxygenation and the health of, and number of, blood cells, so helps to fight fatigue.

Peach energizer

The grapefruit blast in this drink will perk you up and sharpen your senses, while the peach will provide natural sugars to boost your energy levels, and the ginger will soothe and comfort. It's so much better for you than a cup of tea and a chocolate cookie!

Serves 1

* 1 pink or ruby grapefruit, zest and a little pith removed, halved
* 1 carrot, halved
* ½-inch piece of fresh ginger
* 1 large peach, pitted and coarsely chopped
* 1 tablespoon light tahini
* ½ cup chilled water (optional)
* small handful of crushed ice

Make it peachy

Feed the grapefruit and then the carrot and ginger through a juicer. Pour the juice into a blender, add the peach, tahini, water (if using), and crushed ice, and blend until smooth. Pour into a glass and serve immediately.

Peach
energizer

Plum power

This pretty, icy fruit shake will cool you down while giving you a quick burst of energy from the plums and honey and more sustainable energy from the yogurt.

Serves 1

* 2 plums, halved and pitted
* ½ cup water
* 2 teaspoons honey
* 2 scoops of plain frozen yogurt
* 1 Italian almond or pistachio biscotti, crumbled, to decorate (optional)
* ¼ plum, pitted, to decorate (optional)

Ice, ice baby

Put the plums, water, and honey in a small saucepan over medium heat. Stir, cover tightly, reduce the heat to low, and simmer for 15 minutes, until the plums have split and are soft. Let cool. Pour the mixture into a blender, add the frozen yogurt, and blend until smooth. Pour into a glass, sprinkle with the biscotti (if using), decorate the rim with the plum (if using), and serve immediately.

Plums for vitamin C

Plums are a great source of vitamin C, which helps you to fight infection and increase iron absorption. But don't eat too many at once, because they are known to have a laxative effect.

Boost brain power

After intense concentration or physical exercise, energy levels plummet. Not having enough glucose in the blood makes us feel weak and tired. Glucose enables good concentration and focus. However, once your blood glucose is in the normal range, you cannot boost your brain power further by increasing your glucose levels.

Ginger energizer

The ginger in this oh-so-good-for-you veggie drink will pep you up when you're feeling sluggish.

Serves 1

* 2 carrots, halved
* 4 tomatoes, coarsely chopped
* 1 tablespoon lemon juice
* ½ cup fresh flat-leaf parsley
* 1¼-inch piece of fresh ginger, peeled and finely grated
* small handful of crushed ice (optional)
* ½ cup chilled water

To make this juice

Feed the carrots through a juicer. Pour the juice into a blender, add the tomatoes and lemon juice, and blend. Add the parsley (reserving a sprig to decorate), ginger, and crushed ice, if using, and blend again, until smooth. Add the water and blend again. Pour into a glass, garnish with the parsley sprig, and serve immediately.

Good-for-you ginger

Ginger has been used as a natural remedy for centuries, especially for ailments involving the digestive system. Pregnant women are often encouraged to drink ginger tea to prevent morning sickness. Recent studies have shown that ginger may also help with menstrual cramps, migraines, colds, flu, and heartburn.

Power gulp

Beet is a favorite vegetable among sportsmen and sportswomen. It's great for boosting stamina and making muscles work harder, and it's packed with vitamins, minerals, carbohydrates, protein, and powerful antioxidants. All that's missing is fat, and that's no bad thing!

Serves 1

* 2 beets, halved
* 3 tablespoons flaxseeds
* 4 plums, quartered and pitted
* 1 cup seedless red grapes
* 1 cup chilled water
* ice, to serve (optional)

Give it a whirl

Feed the beets through a juicer. Put the flaxseeds in a blender and blend until finely ground. Add the beet juice, plums, grapes, and water, and blend until smooth. Pour into a glass, add ice (if using), and serve immediately.

Blending bananas

Bananas, like apples, discolor, so
make sure you serve this juice
straight from the blender.

Apple attack

This juice provides a good combination of natural sugars for instant energy and soluble fiber for slow-release energy, and is a great source of protein and calcium for building strong muscles and bones.

Serves 1

* 2 apples, halved
* 1 small banana, peeled and coarsely chopped
* 2 tablespoons plain yogurt
* 1 tablespoon light tahini
* ½ teaspoon sesame seeds, to decorate

How to make it

Feed the apples through a juicer. Pour the juice into a blender, add the banana, yogurt, and tahini, and blend again, until smooth. Pour into a glass, sprinkle with sesame seeds, and serve.

Apples for energy

Apples give a great energy-boosting natural fruit sugar hit. They also contain pectin (the setting agent in preserves), vitamins, and minerals. Pectin helps to remove excess cholesterol and toxic metals from the digestive tract and stimulates friendly bacteria in the large intestine. Perhaps that's why our mothers and grandmas used to say "an apple a day keeps the doctor away."

Muscular magic

It would be easy to believe that just looking at this green drink could make you feel healthier! The good news is that it really is bursting with vitamins and minerals.

Serves 1

* ¾ cup green curly kale
* small handful of fresh flat-leaf parsley
* ½ romaine lettuce
* 2 celery stalks, halved
* 1 apple, halved
* ½ lemon
* ¼ cup slivered almonds
* ½ avocado, pitted and flesh scooped from the skin
* small handful of crushed ice (optional)

To make this juice

Feed the kale, then the parsley and lettuce, and finally the celery, apple, and lemon through a juicer. Put the almonds in a blender and blend until finely ground. Add the kale juice mix and avocado flesh, and blend again, until smooth. Add the crushed ice, if using, and blend again. Pour into a glass and serve immediately.

Post-exercise boost

Nutritionists recommend that after exercise you have a healthy snack within 30 minutes to help promote muscle repair and growth.

Natural apple booster

Feeling stressed and tired? Then enjoy this comforting apple-pie-in-a-glass with a hint of honey and cinnamon. You could try organic brown rice syrup instead of honey for a lighter, nuttier flavor.

Serves 1

* 3 apples, halved
* 2 teaspoons flax oil
* 1 teaspoon honey
* pinch of ground cinnamon
* small handful of crushed ice (optional)
* 1 cinnamon stick (optional)

Mix it up

Feed the apples through a juicer. Pour the juice into a blender, add the flax oil, honey, cinnamon, and crushed ice (if using), and blend. Pour into a glass and serve immediately with the cinnamon stick as a stirrer (if using).

Juicing apples

Apple juice discolors quickly, so make this juice just before you need it. The color of the juice will depend on the color of the apple skins; for a juice with a hint of pink, use red-skinned apples.

Muscular magic

page 102

Natural apple
booster

page 103

Tropical refresher

Papaya and mango are both rich in natural fruit sugars, which give an energy boost. They're easy to digest and gentle on the stomach.

Serves 1

* 1 banana, peeled and coarsely chopped
* ½ papaya, peeled, seeded, and coarsely chopped
* ½ mango, pitted, peeled, and coarsely chopped
* 1 lime, juice squeezed
* ¾-inch piece of fresh ginger, peeled and finely grated
* 2 teaspoons hemp oil
* ½ cup unsweetened rice, almond, or soy milk
* small handful of crushed ice

For a tropical island dream ...

Put the banana, papaya, and mango in a blender, and blend until smooth. Add the lime, ginger, hemp oil, milk, and crushed ice, and blend again. Pour into a glass and serve immediately.

Superfood: kale

From shiny blue-green to red, this ruffled, leafy vegetable boasts a healthy amount of calcium, vitamin B, vitamin C, and beta-carotene. The antioxidant lutein helps to protect us from macular eye degeneration, while indoles offer protection against estrogen-related cancers, and sulforaphane may help boost the liver's ability to detoxify carcinogenic compounds. In 1939, the British government encouraged people in the UK to grow kale in the "Dig for Victory" campaign because it is easy for even a novice gardener to grow and is highly nutritious.

Cranberry & pineapple fatigue buster

This fruit combination works really well, with the natural sweetness of the pineapple balancing the sharpness of the cranberries. It can be made in advance and taken to a gym session in a thermos to give an energizing boost to valuable glycogen stores pre- and post-exercise.

Serves 1

* ¼ cup chia seeds
* ½ small pineapple, peeled and coarsely chopped
* 1 cup cranberries
* small handful of ice (optional)

Give it a whirl

Put the chia seeds in a blender and blend until finely ground. Add the pineapple and cranberries, and blend again, until smooth. Fill a glass halfway with ice, if using, pour in the juice, and serve immediately.

Belly-soothing pineapple

Rich in energy-boosting fruit sugars and vitamin C, pineapple also contains the digestive enzyme bromelain, which can have a calming effect on the stomach and so help anyone who feels nauseous after a strenuous workout or marathon run. It is also thought to act as an anti-inflammatory agent to accelerate tissue repair, and so it may help to aid the recovery of bruising, blisters, and sprains.

Preparing pineapples

Juicers have different-sized motors. Those with a smaller motor may not be able to cope with pineapple skin, which is why it is cut off in this book. Check your manual and see if you need to cut the skin off before juicing.

Green energy

This supersmoothie is packed with antioxidants, vitamins, and minerals. The spirulina is a great protein-booster, too.

Serves 1

* 1 pear, halved
* ¼ cucumber, roughly chopped
* 1½ cups young spinach
* 4 sprigs of fresh flat-leaf parsley
* ½ avocado, pitted and flesh scooped from the skin
* ½ teaspoon spirulina powder
* chilled water, to taste
* 1 brazil nut, coarsely chopped

Mix it up

Feed the pear and cucumber through a juicer. Pour the juice into a blender, add the spinach, parsley, and avocado, and blend until smooth. Pour into a glass. Mix the spirulina with just enough water to make a thick liquid, then swirl it into the juice. Sprinkle with the chopped brazil nut, then serve.

Ripening avocados

Just-ripe avocados will have the best flavor. If you have one that is slightly underripe, put it in a brown paper bag and store it in a warm place, such as on a sunny windowsill, to help it ripen.

Avocado benefits

Avocados may inhibit the growth of prostate cancer and, being high in oleic acid, may also help to prevent breast cancer. They contain more of the carotenoid lutein than any other commonly consumed fruit. Lutein protects against macular degeneration and cataracts, two disabling age-related eye diseases. Eating avocados may also lower your cholesterol levels and, as an excellent source of glutathione, they even contain antiaging properties.

Mango & lime bone-builder

This pretty, green-speckled drink looks mango-free, but the fruit's natural sweetness balances the kale, and its flavor comes through even if its color is disguised.

Serves 1

* 1 tablespoon sesame seeds
* ½ lime, juice squeezed
* ½ cup green curly kale pieces
* 1 mango, pitted, peeled, and coarsely chopped
* 1 cup unsweetened rice, almond, or soy milk
* small handful of crushed ice

Give it a whirl

Put the sesame seeds in a blender and blend until finely ground. Add the lime juice, kale, and mango, and blend until blended. Add the milk and crushed ice, and blend again, until smooth. Pour into a glass and serve immediately.

Good for your bones

Calcium-boosting sesame seeds, kale, and fortified soy milk all help to maintain bone strength and function of the nerves and muscles. The addition of vitamin D to the soy milk aids absorption.

Grape & lychee reviver

Go Asian with fragrant lychees, thought by the Chinese to be the symbol of love. Blend them with creamy, smooth avocado and naturally sweet grapes for the perfect pick-me-up to rehydrate and fight fatigue.

Serves 1

* 2 cups green grapes
* 2 cups young spinach
* ½ ripe avocado, pitted and flesh scooped from the skin, plus a slice to serve (optional)
* 5 lychees, peeled and pitted
* small handful of crushed ice (optional)
* ½ cup chilled water

Blend it up

Feed the grapes and spinach through a juicer. Pour the juice into a blender, add the avocado, lychees, and crushed ice, if using, and blend until smooth. Add the water and blend again. Pour into a glass, add the avocado slice (if using), and serve immediately.

Grape nutrition

Grapes are a good source of potassium, although weight for weight they provide only one-twentieth of the vitamin C of kiwis. The Greeks regarded them as an aphrodisiac, and they are the fruit of Dionysus, the Greek god of fertility and procreation.

Superpowered mango

You don't need to be a sportsman or sportswoman to benefit from an energy boost; coping with a young family can be just as tiring! Instead of reaching for a chocolate cookie or slice of cake to pick you up in the middle of the afternoon, try this energizing fruit blend of clementines, mango, and apples. If clementines are out of season, you can use an orange.

Serves 1

* 2 clementines, zest and a little pith removed
* 1 mango, pitted and peeled
* 2 apples, halved
* small handful of ice (optional)
* chilled water, to taste
* 1 teaspoon honey

How to make this juice

Feed the clementines, mango, and apples through a juicer. Fill a glass halfway with ice (if using). Pour in the juice, add water to taste, stir in the honey, and serve immediately.

How to prepare mango

Cut a thick slice off the top of the mango, using a sharp knife, then cut one off the bottom to reveal a large, flattish oval pit. Cut around the pit, keeping all the trimmings. Push out the skin, cut the flesh into cubes, then cut the cubes off the skin.

Mango for energy
A mango is 14 percent natural sugar, and this can be quickly converted into energy by the body. It is also rich in beta-carotene and vitamin C.

Health

Fruit & veg nutrition

Your weight, energy levels, complexion, and mood are all influenced by the foods you eat. Making smart dietary choices can help to protect and restore your health. Here's a guide to the nutrition of fruit and vegetables.

Apples, pears & plums

These orchard fruits are good sources of vitamin C, soluble pectin (which is thought to help lower cholesterol), and the minerals calcium, magnesium, and phosphorus.

Tropical fruit

When it comes to mango, papaya, melon, and pineapple, the stronger the color of the fruit, the more healthy carotenoids it will contain, including beta-carotene. These fruits are also rich in vitamin C.

Berries

Strawberries, raspberries, blackberries, and blueberries are good sources of vitamin C and fiber. The different fruits contain varying amounts of vitamin K, the B vitamins, and minerals and have antiviral and antibacterial properties. Good antioxidants may help to lower cholesterol.

Bananas

Bananas are rich in complex carbohydrates to boost energy, potassium to regulate blood pressure, and tryptophan and vitamin B6 to boost serotonin (the good mood chemical).

What counts as a portion?

Health professionals recommend that you eat at least five portions of fresh fruit and vegetables each day. One 5-fluid-ounce or more glass of fruit or vegetable juice made in a juicer counts as one of your five-a-day. But even if you drink several glasses, they will still only count as one portion. However, two 5-fluid-ounce glasses of fruit smoothie (as opposed to juices) can count as two of your five a day, because they are blended instead of juiced and so often contain the whole fruit, which means more fiber, antioxidants, and other nutrients should be present. But if you drink more than two smoothies per day, they will still only count as two of your five-a-day.

Broccoli & kale

Kale and broccoli are two of the most well-known superfoods, rich in antioxidants, vitamins C and K, calcium, magnesium, and zinc.

Green leafy vegetables

Spinach, Swiss chard, romaine lettuce, and watercress are rich in the vitamin B complex, needed to make serotonin (a mood-boosting chemical). They are also loaded with antioxidants to help reduce the risk of heart disease and cancer. They contain lutein, a carotenoid antioxidant that helps protect against cataracts and macular degeneration, and a good mix of minerals.

Root veggies

Root vegetables, such as beets, carrots, sweet potatoes, and parsnips, are the storage organs of the plants they support. They are packed with fiber, starch, and sugar, so they are good for boosting energy. They also contain vitamins and minerals, antioxidants, and phytonutrients.

Onions, leeks & garlic

Sulfur compounds found in onions, leeks, and garlic help us to relax and enlarge blood vessels to reduce blood pressure. Allicin in garlic and onions is antibacterial and antiviral and may help us fight colds, flu, stomach viruses, and candida yeast. They can also help reduce inflammation, so may relieve arthritis and protect against asthma attacks.

Avocados

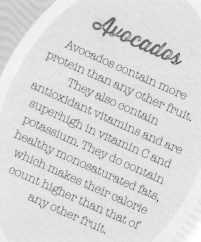

Avocados contain more protein than any other fruit. They also contain antioxidant vitamins and are superhigh in vitamin C and potassium. They do contain healthy monosaturated fats, which makes their calorie count higher than that of any other fruit.

Antioxidants explained

A lot of fruit and vegetables contain antioxidants. These may be an important part of the diet and involved in DNA and cell maintenance and repair. Vitamins C and E are antioxidants, as are the minerals zinc and selenium. It is thought antioxidants may help reduce the production of free radicals, preventing early damage to cells and potentially reducing the incidence of cancer, heart disease, and brain function decline.

A helping hand

While it's great to make a juice with a mixture of different fruits and vegetables, sometimes you just don't have the time or the ingredients in the refrigerator. These three quick juices all consist of just one ingredient plus a supplement to boost their nutrient values.

1

Apple & spirulina

* 2 apples, halved
* 1 teaspoon spirulina powder

Spirulina

This dark green algae has 10 times more calcium than milk, and 58 times more iron than spinach. It contains 60 percent protein and is rich in essential fatty acids and vitamin B12. (Also see page 70.)

Serves 1

For each of these drinks, feed the fruit or vegetable through a juicer, then pour the juice into a screw-top jar. Add the powder, screw on the lid, and shake really well, so that the finished drink doesn't taste powdery. Pour into a glass and serve immediately.

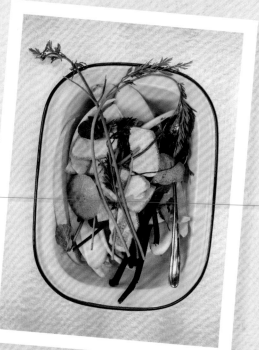

2

Carrot & baobab

* 4 carrots, halved
* 1 teaspoon baobab powder

Baobab

Baobab is an African fruit that has six times more potassium than bananas, six times more vitamin C than oranges, six times more antioxidants than blueberries, twice as many antioxidants as goji berries, and twice as much calcium as milk.

Ripe pears

Don't worry if the pears are a little hard; you will still be able to extract plenty of juice.

Pears for immunity

Pears contain antioxidants, including vitamin C and copper. Antioxidants encourage a strong immune system and help our bodies to fight off disease and illness.

3

Pear & wheatgrass

* 2 pears, halved
* 1 teaspoon wheatgrass powder

Wheatgrass

Wheatgrass contains all eight essential amino acids. It also contains vitamins E, K, and B complex (especially B_{12}) and chlorophyll and is rich in calcium, vitamin C, and iron. Freshly juiced wheatgrass is the best for you, but wheatgrass powder makes a quick, convenient alternative and is a great pantry standby.

Cranberry soother

Help to protect your body with this wonderfully colorful and tasty drink. It's a great way to encourage your children to eat more vitamin-C-packed fruit, too.

Serves 1

* 1½ cups cranberries
* 1 orange, juice squeezed
* ⅓ cup plain yogurt
* 2 teaspoons honey

Cool cranberries

Cranberries contain significant amounts of antioxidants and other phytonutrients that may help protect against heart disease and cancer. As well as helping to prevent infections of the urinary tract, they are thought to be beneficial to the health of your heart and teeth. They may also help prevent ulcers and are thought to have antiaging properties.

Blend it up

Put the cranberries and orange juice in a blender, and blend until smooth. Add the yogurt and honey, and blend again. Pour into a glass and serve.

Up the anti

Protect your body from the inside out with this fresh, fruity drink that is bursting with antioxidants, your body's defense team.

Serves 1

* ½ avocado, pitted and flesh scooped from the skin
* 1 cup blueberries
* ¾ cup hulled strawberries
* 1 tangerine or small orange, juice squeezed
* ½ cup chilled water
* small handful of crushed ice (optional)

To make this juice

Put the avocado, blueberries, strawberries, tangerine juice, and water in a blender and blend. Add the crushed ice (if using) and blend again, until smooth. Pour into a glass and serve.

Soothing smoothie

Cranberries are soothing for the digestive and urinary tracts. They are also a good source of cancer-fighting phytochemicals. This smoothie is packed with vitamin C, plus potassium for regulating blood pressure.

Serves 1

* 1 orange
* ½ cup cranberries
* 1 banana, peeled and coarsely chopped
* ½ cup soy yogurt

Go bananas!

Cut the zest from the orange and finely shred and reserve a little of it; discard the rest. Remove the seeds and most of the pith, and discard them. Coarsely chop the flesh and put it and the cranberries in a blender, then blend. Add the banana and yogurt, and blend again, until smooth. Pour into a glass, sprinkle with the shredded orange zest, and serve.

Sweet banana

Once bananas have brown speckles on the skin, they become naturally sweeter and easier to digest. When combined with protein-rich soy yogurt as in this drink, they provide a more sustaining, longer-lasting energy fix.

Stress buster

Ginseng is a natural stimulant that helps to combat stress and lifts the mood. This teatime juice also aids liver and kidney function and prevents fluid retention.

Serves 1

* 1 ginseng tea bag or 1 teaspoon ginseng tea
* 1 cup boiling water
* 1 apple, halved
* 2 cups arugula leaves

Time for tea

Put the tea bag in a cup, pour the boiling water over it, and let stand for 4 minutes. Strain the water into a glass. Feed the apple and then the arugula through a juicer. Stir the juice into the tea and serve warm or cold.

Looking after your skin

Give yourself a facial from the inside out with this drink. Every skin pore eliminates waste and sweat, and the sebaceous glands help to remove toxins. The skin reflects what is happening inside our bodies; if we are stressed, run down, or have overdone things a little, our skin will look tired and lifeless, with pimples and blemishes.

The glory of ginseng

Ginseng is a slow-growing plant with fleshy roots. It typically grows in northern China, Korea, and eastern Siberia. As well as being believed to be a powerful aphrodisiac and tonic, it may also act as an appetite suppressant, which can help to encourage weight loss. Ginseng tea is additionally believed to be effective against menstrual stomach pain.

Parsley purifier

As a diuretic, this drink really helps to purify your body. The strong flavors of the herbs and spinach are balanced by the natural sweetness of the sugar snap peas and the deliciously delicate flavor of the cucumber.

Serves 1

* 2 cups sugar snap peas
* small handful of fresh flat-leaf parsley
* 2 sprigs of fresh rosemary
* 1 garlic clove
* 2 cups young spinach
* ½ cucumber
* 2 celery stalks, halved
* 1 teaspoon hemp oil
* chilled water, to taste
* ice, to serve (optional)

Give it a whirl

Feed the sugar snap peas, parsley (reserving 1 sprig to garnish), rosemary, and garlic, then the spinach, and finally, the cucumber and celery through a juicer. Pour into a glass, stir in the hemp oil and water to taste, garnish with the parsley sprig, and serve with ice (if using).

Take a fresh look at celery, parsley & rosemary

Celery has been used as a diuretic for centuries and helps to flush excess fluid from the body. It also contains phthalides, which have been shown to lower blood pressure by relaxing muscles around the arteries, allowing blood vessels to dilate. Celery contains calcium, magnesium, and potassium, which help regulate blood pressure. Parsley is rich in calcium and potassium, too, and has a lot of iron, phosphorus, and sodium. Just 2 tablespoons of parsley contain a whopping 153 percent of the recommended daily allowance of vitamin K (which works with protein to help strengthen bones, and helps prevent the buildup of calcium in tissues that can lead to atherosclerosis, cardiovascular disease, and stroke). Used by herbalists for centuries, rosemary also acts as a diuretic. It is anti-inflammatory and antiseptic, too, and can help to calm digestive pains.

Ginger pep-up

Pretty and fragrant, with the warmth of ginger, this juice will brighten a less-than-perfect summer's day.

Serves 1

* 2 pears, halved
* 4 oranges, juice squeezed
* 4 cubes of crystallized ginger

Spice things up

Feed the pears through a juicer. Pour the juice into a blender, add the orange juice and crystallized ginger, and blend until smooth. Pour into a glass and serve.

Pears for health

Fresh pear juice, rich in natural fruit sugars, takes the edge off the sharpness of citrus juice. Pears have a high water content, and their pectin helps to lower cholesterol and acts as a diuretic and mild laxative. They also contain flavanoids. Cloudy pear juice contains 40 percent more phenolic phytonutrients and more antioxidants than filtered clear pear juice.

Stomach soother

Pineapple juice is great for improving digestion and soothing an upset stomach. The healing enzyme bromelain reduces bruising, so it can help with recovery from an injury. It's also a good source of vitamin C, which helps to heal and fight infection.

Serves 1

* ½ sweet pineapple, peeled and cut into thick slices, plus a leaf to decorate
* 1 lemon, zest and most of the pith removed, halved
* ¾-inch piece of fresh ginger

On your marks, get set, go!

Feed the pineapple, lemon, and ginger through a juicer. Pour into a glass and add a pineapple leaf as a stirrer, if you desire. Remove the pineapple leaf before drinking.

Green goddess

This cooling, cleansing drink is good for liver and kidney function, helps lower cholesterol, and relieves tension and insomnia. It's high in iron and chlorophyll, which benefits your eyes and helps maintain healthy blood vessels.

Serves 1

* ½ honeydew melon, thickly sliced and peel removed
* 3 cups young spinach
* 2 large sprigs of fresh flat-leaf parsley
* 3 large sprigs of fresh mint
* small handful of ice (optional)

Time to juice

Feed the melon, then the spinach, parsley, and 2 sprigs of mint through a juicer. Fill a glass halfway with ice (if using), then pour in the juice, garnish with the remaining sprig of mint, and serve immediately.

Crimson vitality

Good health depends on every cell in the body receiving its fair share of nutrition. Your blood absorbs vital nutrition and circulates around the body. What better or easier way for the body to digest vital vitamins and minerals than through this vitality-boosting beet juice?

Serves 1

* 1 beet, halved
* 1 cup cranberries
* ½-inch piece of fresh ginger
* 2 apples, halved
* small handful of ice (optional)
* chilled water, to taste

In the pink ...

Feed the beet, then the cranberries and ginger, and finally the apples through a juicer. Fill a glass halfway with ice (if using), pour in the juice, add water to taste, and serve immediately.

Use the beet leaves!

If your beet has fresh, vibrant leaves instead of tired, limp-looking ones, add them to the juicer, too.

Superfood: beets

Beets are packed with minerals, vitamins, carbohydrates, protein, fiber, and antioxidants. When betacyanin, the pigment that gives beets their color, combines with carotenoids and flavonoids and is consumed regularly, it is believed that it may help reduce the oxidation of LDL cholesterol. This in turn protects artery walls and reduces the risk of heart disease and strokes. Recent research has found that regular intake of beet juice helps to lower high blood pressure. Beets are also rich in potassium and folic acid and contain iron, so are good for those with anemia or fatigue. Their high levels of nitrites have been shown to benefit sportsmen and sportswomen and may even help to slow the progression of dementia.

Spring clean

This dark-color juice tastes surprisingly light and fresh. The wheatgrass has long been associated with healing properties.

Serves 1

* 1½ large broccoli florets
* 2 apples, halved
* 1 zucchini, halved
* 1 teaspoon wheatgrass powder
* small handful of ice (optional)

To make this juice

Feed the broccoli, then the apples and zucchini through a juicer. Add the wheatgrass powder and whisk until smooth. Fill a glass halfway with ice, if using, pour in the juice, and serve immediately.

Wonderful wheatgrass

Modern medics have mixed views on the health benefits of wheatgrass. Yes, it is rich in chlorophyll and protein and contains vitamins A, C, E, K, and B$_{12}$ plus a range of minerals, but nothing else is certain. Some homeopaths believe that it may help reduce the side effects of chemotherapy. You can find it for sale in health food stores.

Body balancer

Look quickly at this drink and you could mistake it for a coffee swirled with hot milk, but it is actually dairy-free and caffeine-free. The prunes make it a natural laxative.

Serves 1

* 1 tablespoon flaxseed
* 8 pitted prunes
* 1 small banana, peeled and coarsely chopped
* 1 tablespoon wheat germ
* 2 large oranges, juice squeezed
* 1½ cup vanilla soy yogurt
* 1 cup chilled water

Blend it up

Put the flaxseed in a blender and blend until finely ground. Add the prunes, banana, and wheat germ, and blend again. Add the orange juice and half the yogurt, and blend again, until smooth. Add the water and blend once more. Pour into a glass, add the remaining yogurt, and swirl together with a teaspoon, then serve.

A natural laxative

Prunes are one of the most effective laxatives. They are rich in potassium, which is needed for the healthy function of cells, nerves, and muscles and to regulate blood pressure. The natural cultures in the yogurt in this drink help restore the balance of healthy bacteria in your digestive tract.

Spring clean
page 144

Body balancer
page 145

Multimineral bonanza

With spinach, beets, oranges, and carrots, this drink provides a bumper beta-carotene and vitamin C hit.

Serves 1

* 2 beets, halved
* 1½ cups young spinach
* 2 carrots, halved
* 2 oranges, zest and a little pith removed, halved
* 1 tablespoon sesame seeds, finely ground
* small handful of ice (optional)
* sparkling mineral water, chilled, to taste

Mix it up!

Feed the beets, spinach, and carrots, then the oranges through a juicer. Stir in the ground sesame seeds. Fill a glass halfway with ice, if using, then pour in the juice, fill up with sparkling water to taste, and serve immediately.

Red pepper reviver

This fiery juice is sure to wake you up if you're having
a midmorning snooze!

Serves 1

* 2 carrots, halved, plus strips
  of shredded carrot to garnish
* 2 tomatoes, halved
* 1 large red bell pepper, halved
* 2 teaspoons lemon juice
* freshly ground black pepper

On your marks, get set, go!

Feed the carrots, then the tomatoes and red
bell pepper through a juicer. Stir in the lemon
juice and plenty of black pepper. Pour into
a glass, garnish with the strips of shredded
carrot, and serve.

Thumbs up for tomatoes

Tomatoes are rich in lycopene, a
carotenoid pigment that turns them
red. It is thought this may help prevent
some forms of cancer. They are also a
good source of potassium, with smaller
amounts of vitamins C and E. They
contain 90 percent water, so are great for
rehydration, too.

Cutting calories

The more you get into juicing, the less
appealing that takeout snack will be.
Just cutting down 100 or 200 calories
a day can have a big impact on your
weight over the course of a year.

Red pep-up

Full of disease-fighting, antiaging antioxidants, this drink provides a lot of energy from its natural sweetness to help you get through the day.

Serves 1

* 2 fennel bulbs with leaves, halved
* 1 apple, halved
* 1 small red bell pepper, halved
* 1 carrot, halved

Give it a whirl

Remove a few leaves from the fennel and reserve. Feed the apple, then the fennel and bell pepper, and finally the carrot through a juicer. Pour into a glass, garnish with the fennel leaves, and serve.

Winter pick-me-up

Banish the winter blues with this nutrient-packed juice that boosts vitamin, mineral, and energy levels.

Serves 1

* 1 parsnip, halved
* 2 carrots, halved, plus 2 carrot sticks to garnish
* 1 garlic clove
* 2 apples, halved
* 2 tablespoons rolled oats
* 1 tablespoon wheat germ
* 2 teaspoons honey
* small handful of ice (optional)

How to use wheat germ

Wheat germ flakes swell in your drinks. This means that if you don't serve a juice or smoothie as soon as you have made it, you will need to add a splash of chilled water to return it to the right consistency.

Blend it up

Feed the parsnip, carrots, and garlic, then the apples through a juicer. Put the oats and wheat germ in a blender, and blend until finely ground. Add the honey and parsnip juice mix, and blend again, until smooth. Fill a glass halfway with ice (if using). Pour in the juice, add the carrot sticks, and serve immediately.

Buying parsnips

Buy parsnips a few weeks after the first frost if you can, because much of the starch is converted to sugar in a frost, making them taste sweeter.

Detox

Beet aid detox

This thirst-quenching, nutrient-packed juice is bursting with vitamins and minerals. Since Roman times, beets have been thought of as an aphrodisiac, so who knows what might happen when you feel detoxed and reenergized?

Serves 1

* 1 beet, halved
* ½ lime
* 4 red Swiss chard leaves
* 1½ pounds watermelon, cut into 3 thicks slices and peel removed
* small handful of ice (optional)

Smoothie steps

Feed the beet and lime, then the Swiss chard and watermelon through a juicer. Fill a glass halfway with ice (if using), then pour in the juice and serve immediately.

Health notes

Beets contain virtually all the vitamins and minerals needed to give your whole body a boost. Watermelon's high water content helps to rehydrate and plump up your skin.

Citrus cleanser

Citrus fruits stimulate the digestive system. In traditional folk medicine, it was thought they also acted as a cleanser and astringent, stimulating the liver and gallbladder.

Serves 1

* 1 pink or ruby grapefruit, zest and a little pith removed, halved
* 1 orange, zest and a little pith removed, halved
* 1 lime, zest and pith removed from half
* 1 large pear, halved
* small handful of ice (optional)

To make this juice

Feed the grapefruit, orange, and lime, then the pear through a juicer. Fill a glass halfway with ice (if using), pour in the juice, and serve immediately.

Grapefruit nutrition

Grapefruit is a great source of vitamin C. It is also packed with flavonoids (natural chemical compounds that may reduce early damage to DNA and cell membranes).

Pears to add sweetness

Grapefruit and lime juices can be a little sharp for some tastes, even when mixed with orange juice. Fresh pear juice, which is rich in natural fruit sugars, takes the edge off this sharpness. High in water, pear helps to rehydrate the body. The pectin in pears helps to lower cholesterol and acts as a diuretic and mild laxative.

Juicing pears
Pears oxidate, losing their flavor,
soon after juicing, so serve this juice
as soon as you have made it.

Cucumber spring clean

Think of this as a chilled gingered gazpacho, and you can enjoy the detox qualities of ginger and onion for a light lunch. If you drink it outside in the sunshine, you could almost feel transported to a Mediterranean terrace.

Serves 1

* ½ romaine lettuce
* 2 tomatoes
* ¾-inch piece of fresh ginger
* 1 scallion
* 1 celery stalk, halved
* 1 carrot, halved
* ¼ cucumber, plus a slice to garnish (optional)
* small handful of ice (optional)

Blend it up

Feed the lettuce and tomatoes, then the ginger, scallion, celery, carrot, and cucumber through a juicer. Fill a glass halfway with ice (if using), pour in the juice, add the cucumber slice to garnish (if using), and serve immediately.

Love your lettuce

Lettuces contain the latexlike compound lactucarium, which is thought to calm and soothe the nerves and aid sleep. They are about 90 percent water. The outer leaves supply the most beta-carotene, vitamin C, folate, and iron.

Know your onions

Onions, leeks, and garlic are rich in antiviral and antibacterial nutrients that are thought to cleanse the system. They are most potent when eaten raw, but use just a little because they have a strong flavor.

Lettuce choice

If you don't have a romaine lettuce, choose cos or iceberg. Boston lettuce would also work, but you will need to use two of them.

Green jump-start

If you like spinach or watercress soup, you will love this juice. You don't get a huge amount of juice from these green leaves, but what you do get is concentrated with antioxidants, minerals, and vitamins. Mix them with thirst-quenching zucchini and apples for a health boost that will jump-start your detox.

Serves 1

* 2 cups young spinach
* 1 cup watercress
* 1 zucchini, halved
* 2 apples, halved
* 1 teaspoon wheatgrass powder (optional)
* small handful of ice (optional)

Give it a whirl

Feed the spinach and watercress, then the zucchini and apples through a juicer. Stir in the wheatgrass powder (if using). Fill a glass halfway with ice (if using), pour in the juice, and serve immediately.

Get into good habits

A detox can help you review your eating habits. Most of us don't eat enough green vegetables, and this tasty juice is a way to increase your consumption easily.

Broccoli & parsley revitalizer

Wonderfully soothing and gentle, this delicate, revitalizing green juice is naturally sweet and refreshing, and makes a perfect alternative to a caffeine-loaded tea or coffee in the afternoon.

Serves 1

* 1½ cups large broccoli florets
* small handful of fresh flat-leaf parsley
* ½ fennel bulb
* 2 apples, halved
* chilled water, to taste
* small handful of ice (optional)

Fire up your juicer

Feed the broccoli and parsley, then the fennel and apples through a juicer. Add water to taste. Fill a glass halfway with ice (if using), pour in the juice, and serve immediately.

Fabulous fennel

Fennel acts as a diuretic and has a calming effect on the stomach while providing useful amounts of beta-carotene and folate. Parsley is also a diuretic, and herbalists have long believed it helps reduce inflammation in the kidneys and bladder.

Papaya & apricot soother

Papaya and apricots blend to a wonderfully silky, smooth texture that feels soothing, especially if you are battling a sore throat. This smoothie is packed with vitamin C to help fight off the symptoms of colds and flu.

Serves 1

* ½ papaya, peeled, seeded, and coarsely chopped
* 4 apricots, pitted
* 2 oranges, juice squeezed
* 1 lime, juice squeezed
* small handful of crushed ice (optional)
* ¼ cup chilled water

Mix it up

Put the papaya, apricots, and orange and lime juices in a blender, and blend until smooth. Add the crushed ice (if using) and water, and blend again. Pour into a glass and serve immediately.

Best drinks for the morning

Serious fans of detoxing diets recommend that you drink fruit juices in the morning, because they believe these have a stronger detoxifying effect than vegetable juices. Fruit juices do have a mild laxative effect—and because the papaya and apricots are blended instead of juiced in this drink, it also contains soluble fiber that will help keep your digestive system moving and expel cholesterol from your body.

Broccoli & parsley
revitalizer
page 164

Papaya & apricot
soother
page 165

Red cabbage digestive aid

You will be amazed at the vibrant purple juice that comes from a red cabbage. While this drink might look a little like a witch's brew, it is far from wicked. It is light and aromatic, with a hint of cardamom (said to calm digestion) and the delicate sweetness of red grapes.

Serves 1

* 1 cup red grapes
* ½ fennel bulb
* ¼ red cabbage, coarsely chopped
* 3 cardamom pods
* chilled water, to taste
* small handful of ice (optional)

Time to get started

Feed the grapes, then the fennel, and finally the red cabbage through a juicer. Coarsely crush the cardamom using a pestle in a mortar, discard the pods, and then finely crush the black seeds and stir them into the juice. Add water to taste. Fill a glass halfway with ice (if using), pour in the juice, and serve immediately.

Big apple detox

With its creamy, delicate flavor and cleansing ginger, this juice is perfect for after an indulgent holiday or Christmas.

Serves 1

* 1 parsnip, halved
* ¼-inch piece of fresh ginger
* 2 apples, halved
* ½ cup chilled water
* small handful of ice (optional)

Give it a whirl

Feed the parsnip and ginger, then the apples through a juicer. Add the water. Fill a glass halfway with ice (if using), pour in the juice, and serve immediately.

Fresh is best

Instead of buying commercially made detox compounds or potions, freshly juice fruit and vegetables at home. Look at what you eat and when; you might find that making small changes will have a big impact. Ditch that high-calorie, high-fat coffee latte or cola and have a low-calorie, high-vitamin, and high-mineral juice instead.

Nature's remedy

This drink tastes surprisingly mild, with a natural sweetness from the parsnip and carrots, and boy-oh-boy does it do you good!

Serves 1

* 2 carrots, halved
* ½ small onion
* 1 garlic clove
* 1 parsnip, halved
* 1 orange, zest and a little pith removed, halved
* ½ cup chilled water
* pinch of ground turmeric
* pinch of freshly ground black pepper
* small handful of ice (optional)

On your marks, get set, go!

Cut a thin slice from a carrot and reserve. Feed the remaining carrots and the onion, garlic, parsnip, and then the orange through a juicer. Stir in the water, turmeric, and pepper. Fill a glass halfway with ice (if using), pour in the juice, garnish with the carrot slice, and serve.

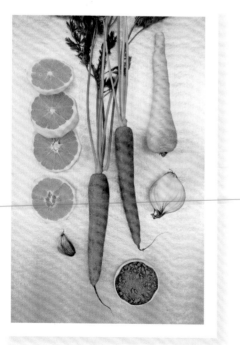

Turmeric's healing properties

Turmeric, a relation of ginger, has long been used in Chinese medicine to help treat depression. It is a natural antiseptic and antibacterial agent. However, it's the anti-inflammatory properties that may be of the most interest—they may help people with arthritis, soothe inflammatory skin infections, such as psoriasis, and according to one study, help to reduce the incidence of Alzheimer's.

Superfoods: carrots

Studies have shown that a diet rich in carotenoids (the pigment that makes carrots orange) may help lower the risk of heart disease, while the soluble fiber that carrots contain can help lower blood cholesterol. Their high level of beta-carotene is converted by the body into vitamin A and helps maintain good eye health and the ability of our eyes to adjust quickly to changes in light. In traditional medicine, carrots were known for their detoxifying properties and for helping to beat acne. For those trying to keep wrinkles at bay, vitamin A is thought to nourish the skin and help fight the signs of aging; it is even added to some beauty creams. But before you overdose on carrot juice, keep in mind that too many carrots can make your skin turn a little orange.

Grape nutrient-booster

Naturally sweet grapes are a good way to disguise the taste of nutritious vegetables, such as cabbage, in a juice. Because the pumpkin seeds in this drink are finely ground, no one will know they are there, either!

Serves 1

* 2 pears, halved
* ¼ small savoy or green cabbage, coarsely chopped
* 1 tablespoon pumpkin seeds
* 1 cup green seedless grapes
* small handful of crushed ice (optional)

Blend it up

Feed the pears and cabbage through a juicer. Put the pumpkin seeds in a blender and blend until finely ground, then add the grapes and crushed ice (if using), and blend again. Pour in the pear juice mix and blend until smooth. Pour into a glass and serve immediately.

Cabbage nutrition

You may have heard about the seven-day cabbage diet to help you detox and shed weight, but you may not know that savoy cabbage (part of the same family as kale, Brussels sprouts, and broccoli) has long been a favorite in herbal remedies. Savoy cabbage is a storehouse of phytochemicals and powerful antioxidants that are thought to help protect against cancer. It also contains a huge range of vitamins and minerals, not to mention beta-carotene and the amino acid glutamine (an anti-inflammatory). Plus, it may help to reduce bad cholesterol in the blood.

Seed swap
Don't have any pumpkin seeds? Then add a few sesame or sunflower seeds or a small handful of finely ground almonds instead.

Index